A GUIDE
TO MORNING, EVENING
AND NIGHT PRAYER

HOW TO PRAY THE PRAYER OF THE CHURCH

by
Robert Taylerson

*All CTS booklets
are published thanks to the
generous support of its Members*

CATHOLIC TRUTH SOCIETY
PUBLISHERS TO THE HOLY SEE

CONTENTS

GETTING STARTED

One of the beautiful ways in which prayer is growing today is by an ever-increasing number of people in many different places coming together to pray the hours of the Prayer of the Church. Previously these were usually prayed only by priests and religious.

This tutorial is intended for those who are starting to pray the Morning, Evening or Night Prayers of the Church. It is suitable whether you are praying these 'hours' of prayer alone or in community with others. It can be used as a self guide or as a work-book for a small group. Where possible do try to work through and pray with at least one other person. It does help.

A variety of editions and books (Office books) are available which contain Morning, Evening, and Night Prayer of the Church e.g. *Daily Prayer*, *Morning & Evening Prayer*, *Shorter Morning & Evening Prayer*, "Three-Volume Divine Office", and their equivalent American editions (such as *Christian Prayer*). It is hoped that this tutorial will be of use to you, whichever edition or book you pray from. Each lesson should be worked through carefully, and the exercises completed before moving on to the next.

This booklet is a revised edition of the 1993 original, which now contains extra references and websites to further help the reader.

Rob Taylerson, February 2005

'In prayer, united with Jesus - your brother, your friend, your Saviour, your God - you begin to breathe a new atmosphere'

John Paul II

LESSON 1

Introduction to Morning, Evening and Night Prayers

What are they?

They are called 'hours' not because they take sixty minutes each to pray but because they are traditionally prayed at set hours throughout the day. The praying of each hour may take between five and twenty minutes, depending on its contents, the length of silences, and how much is sung.

Morning Prayer, Evening Prayer and Night Prayer are three of the regular sets of prayers from the seven 'hours' of the Prayer of the Church (also called the Divine Office, or Breviary). Each is a collection of psalms, scripture and prayers in a continuing tradition of such prayer from early Christian times. They have their roots in the psalms and daily prayer of the Jewish people, and have developed throughout the history of the Christian Church in monasteries, cathedrals and parishes to the present day. In the last thirty years there has been a great increase in their use by lay people as they are now available in modern languages. Previously they were only prayed in Latin.

Where do they come from?

In Psalm 118 (119), traditionally ascribed to king David, the psalmist writes: "Seven times a day I will praise you!" There is an ancient tradition of reciting set prayers regularly through the day. The full hours of the Divine Office comprise seven sets of prayers.

Sometimes you may hear these hours referred to by their previous names:

1. Matins and Lauds (two separate hours, but often treated as one)
2. Prime (which name comes from the start of the Roman day 6 am)
3. Terce (the third Roman hour 9 am)
4. Sext (the sixth Roman hour 12 noon)
5. None (the ninth Roman hour 3 pm)
6. Vespers (the evening prayer)
7. Compline (the night prayer)

A popular verse in the nineteenth century ran as follows:

At Matins bound, at Prime Reviled
Condemned to death at Tierce;
Nailed to the cross at Sext; at None
His blessed side they pierce.
They take him down at Vesper-time
In grave at Compline lay,
Who henceforth bids the Church observe
The sevenfold hours away.

In addition to the tradition of praying seven times a day is another tradition of praying three times a day. In Psalm 54 (55) the psalmist talks of turning to God three times a day (morning, noon and evening) as does Daniel (*Dn* 6:10). This was originally associated with the three Jewish temple sacrifices each day, but the tradition continues in the Christian Church. Many people who do not have the time or the books to pray all seven hours choose to pray one or more from Morning Prayer, Evening Prayer and Night Prayer. Of these the Church commends Morning and Evening prayer as 'hinges' of prayer around which our spiritual day might revolve.

Outline of Morning, Evening and Night Prayer

Morning Prayer is, in particular, a prayer of praise, consecrating the day to God. It has a strong theme of "Offering our day to God." Its main components are:

Hymn
First Psalm
Old Testament Canticle
Second Psalm
Scripture Reading
Responsory
Benedictus (Gospel Canticle)
Intercessions
Our Father
Concluding Prayer

With **Evening Prayer** the theme of thanksgiving replaces that of offering. Its main components are similar:

Hymn
First Psalm
Second Psalm
New Testament canticle
Scripture Reading
Responsory
Magnificat (Gospel Canticle)
Intercessions
Our Father
Concluding Prayer

Night Prayer centres on reconciliation and readiness to meet Christ, either through his second coming or through death. It contains the following:

Examination of Conscience
Penitential Rite
Hymn
Psalm (sometimes two)
Scripture Reading
Responsory
Nunc Dimittis (Gospel Canticle)
Concluding Prayer

Various other 'trimmings' complete these hours, but it is enough for us to start with the basics, and more will be explained later in greater detail. Meanwhile here is a little more introductory information:

1. The introduction to each hour is the sign of the cross (to remind us of Christ's cross and of the Trinity). When praying any of the gospel canticles it is usual to start by making the sign of the cross. We also remember the Trinity after each psalm and most canticles by praying the 'Glory Be'.

2. A canticle is a text of scripture which can be sung like a psalm but does not come from the book of Psalms found in the bible. Each of our three hours contains a canticle from Luke's gospel. In the morning the gospel canticle is Zechariah's prayer, the Benedictus; in the evening Mary's prayer, the Magnificat; and at night Simeon's prayer, the Nunc Dimittis.

3. Morning and Evening Prayers also contain canticles from non-gospel parts of scripture (from the Old Testament in the morning, coming between the two psalms and from the New Testament in the evening coming after the two psalms).

4. Morning and Evening Prayers also contain a series of intercessions which always concludes with the

'Our Father'. Night Prayer has neither intercessions nor the 'Our Father'.

5. All psalms and canticles are introduced by a short phrase or prayer called an antiphon.

Praying with signs of reverence

Out of reverence for the gospel, the gospel canticles and their antiphons are usually prayed standing. In addition to standing for these texts, those who pray usually stand for the commencing prayers and hymn, and for the intercessions (if present) through to the dismissal. A common practice is to bow the head when the 'Glory Be' is recited.

All of the above signs of reverence are normal when praying formally in a community. They are not absolutely necessary when praying by oneself, or in an informal group; here less ceremony is often more appropriate.

These prayers grow in popularity. They offer a good blend of praise, thanks and intercession, reflection and reconciliation. They keep us at the heart of Christ's body, the Church, in a tradition of prayer spanning the whole history of salvation; and by uniting us with God they sanctify each day.

Exercises

At the end of each lesson will be a few questions or tasks to help you to absorb the contents of the lesson, to put it to use, and to be more confident in praying.

1. Where do traditions of praying three times a day and seven times a day come from?

2. Which parts of the hours are usually prayed seated?

3. What is a canticle? From which parts of scripture do canticles come in Morning, Evening and Night prayer?

4. In which of the hours are the following found?
   a. Thanksgiving
   b. Offering and Consecration
   c. Reconciliation
   d. Old Testament Canticle
   e. Intercessions

Further help and information

A number of internet sites have useful information and resources:

www.universalis.com	(psalms and readings for divine office. non-standard translations for copyright reasons and calendar for the liturgy).
www.liturgyhours.org	(booklets for the hours, USA edition)
www.romanrite.com/ hours.html	(simple introduction to the hours)
www.liturgyny.catholic.org /lithours.htm	(simple introduction to the hours)

LESSON 2

Understanding Your Office Book

The sections of the book

No matter which office book you use to pray Morning, Evening and Night Prayers, you may find it difficult to understand how the different parts of the hours are brought together.

It is a mistake to think of your book as something to read from beginning to end. It is better to see it as containing several distinct sections, each of which has a distinct purpose. Think of a loose-leaf file containing different subjects, a filofax or personal organiser, or a Sunday newspaper with several supplements. You then have a better idea of how your book has been edited and put together. Think of the difference between planning day by day, week by week and year by year. No-one would copy a daily timetable on to each page of a yearly diary. In the same way the Office book avoids undue repetition, while allowing for special celebrations when they come round on the calendar. This lesson is to help you understand how the main sections work together.

1. Four-week Psalter

The core of the book is the psalter (so-called because it contains the Psalms). It is a section which contains quite a few pages, so should be easy to identify. As its name implies it is a sequence which is usually repeated every four weeks.

The four weeks are numbered one to four. In many books the Four-Week psalter section is found either in the middle, or close to the beginning of the book. Look in your own book and identify this section. Put a bookmark at the start and another at the end and flip through it to see what it contains. It is the heart of Morning and Evening Prayers. Take some time to try and understand how it is put together. More information is given towards the end of this lesson, but before then try to work out for yourself how it is used.

There are some ingredients of the hours, mentioned in the previous lesson as belonging to the hours, which this section does not contain; there is no mention of an introduction to the hour, no text for the gospel canticle (and no text for its antiphon on a Sunday), no text for the 'Our Father', no text for a blessing or dismissal at the end. These are found elsewhere. To repeat them in print on each day would make your book too bulky.

2. Psalter for Night Prayer

Night Prayer texts repeat every week, rather than every four weeks, so its sequence is in a separate section of your book (often found shortly after the Four-Week Psalter section). It starts with the Night Prayer texts for Saturday Night (usually called 'Sunday 1 Night Prayer') and the section concludes with Friday night. Put in bookmarks at the beginning and end of this section, flip through it to see what it contains and compare it with the Four-Week Psalter.

3. Frequently Recurring Texts

These are the texts which are used daily, but are not in the Psalter sections. Some books include these either on cards or on the very front and last pages of the book. The complete section may also be found just before the beginning of the Four-Week psalter section. Find them in your book. Look for the following:

Invitatory Antiphon and Psalm

The first Office hour which you pray on any particular day (regardless of which hour it is) is traditionally preceded by what is called the Invitatory. Most 'Frequently Recurring Texts' sections begin with the Invitatory opening 'Lord open our lips' (a small sign of the Cross is made with the thumb on the lips) "... and we shall praise your name". The Invitatory Antiphon and Psalm then follow - their detailed use will be described in a later section.

Other Frequently Recurring Texts

    a. an introduction for use when the invitatory is not used,
    b. the gospel canticles for the different hours
    c. introduction to, and text of, the 'Our Father' and
    d. concluding texts.

Identify each of these and see if you can work out how they blend in with the Psalter. These are some of the 'trimmings' which were mentioned in lesson 1.

4. Sunday of the Year

This section is very short. Try using your book's index to locate it. It contains a different pair of Gospel Canticle antiphons for each of the 34 Ordinary Sundays of the Year (excluding Advent, Christmas, Lent and Eastertide). There is also a concluding prayer for each.

5. Proper of Seasons

This section is longer. Like the previous section it provides special Gospel Canticle antiphons and concluding prayers (for Advent, Christmas, Lent and

Easter). It also gives alternative readings, responsories and invititatory antiphons for these seasons.

6. Hymns

In addition to the hymns in the Four-Week Psalter, all books have a section of Marian Anthems to be sung after Evening or Night Prayer. They may have an extra section, too. Flip through your book and see what you have. (Some books may have a further section of hymns for different seasons, others do not).

7. Calendars (Proper of Saints)

Some celebrations and holy days are so important that they deserve parts of the hours unique to themselves. Different editions of books contain different amounts of texts for these celebrations.

Solemn Feasts

All editions have at least the texts for solemnities such as Trinity Sunday, The Body and Blood of Christ (previously called Corpus Christi) and The Sacred Heart.

General Calendar of Saints

Some editions contain a calendar for all the saints whose memory is celebrated universally in the Church.

National Calendars

The above editions usually also have texts for particular Saints celebration in a particular country. This may be a separate section, which is smaller than the General Calendar.

Check your book to see which of these it contains, and look through quickly to see what is in each section.

8. Commons

Some particular celebrations and occasions share prayers, psalms etc, They are held 'in common'. In order to find these most books have a section of Commons, though these are more extensive in some editions than others. A good example of a Common would be prayers etc shared by the different feasts and memoria of Our Lady. Some books have Commons for various different occasions; celebrations of Apostles, Martyrs, Virgins, Pastors etc. Look in your index and flip through your book to see what Commons it contains. Try to work out on which days you might use them.

A similar example would be in remembrance of someone who has died (In the Office for the Dead). Does your Office book have this?

A few notes on the Four-Week Psalter which you may have discovered when you looked at it earlier:

1. Vigils: A vigil occurs when the celebration of a Sunday or holyday is stretched to include the previous evening. The prayer for Saturday evening is called the Sunday vigil or Sunday Evening Prayer 1.

2. Contents: It contains invitatory antiphons, Psalms, non-gospel canticles, hymns, short scripture readings, short responsory, intercessions, (and often an antiphon for the Benedictus or Magnificat).

3. Headings: The section headings (in most editions) are in capital letters, titles to the Psalms are also in capital letters as are any scripture references.

4. Rubrics: Instructions, if any, are in italics. (These are sometimes called rubrics in the older Office books. They were printed in red ink and always intended to be read and followed, but not spoken).

(Reflections or themes are also printed in italics. Most of the rest is in normal upper and lower case print.)

5. What to speak or sing: The rule-of-thumb is that anything in capitals, in bold type, or in italics should not be read out loud.

6. Antiphons: In some editions there are varied antiphons given for differing seasons of the Church's year, and even Psalms or canticles may differ from the norm on some days in selected seasons.

This concludes the understanding of the sections, the building-blocks of which your Office book is made. By now you should have a good idea of what sections there are in your book, and what you might expect to find in each.

Exercises

1. In what sequence do the following sections come in the Office book which you use? Night Prayer Psalter, FRTs, Four-Week Psalter, Calendar, Commons, Proper of Seasons?

2. What other sections does your Office book have, which are not mentioned in the previous question?

3. What is an Invitatory Psalm, and when is it usually used?

4. Give an example of a feast day on which you might use a Common.

LESSON 3

Where to Start for Evening Prayer

This lesson hopes to bring together the understanding gained from the previous lessons to start to pray an 'easy' Evening Prayer.

Which week am I?

This is a familiar call among those who start to pray the hours. The weeks of the Four-week Psalter are tied in with the liturgical weeks of the Church's year which you come across at Sunday Mass. The Church's year has several sections... Advent, Lent, Eastertide, and the general 34 weeks of the year. Each of these sections has a particular Sunday on which they start (first week of Advent, week on which the Baptism of the Lord is celebrated [week 1 of the year], first week of Lent and Easter Sunday). Each of these corresponds with the first week of the four-week psalter. The cycle then repeats itself, so the relationship between the Sunday of the year, and the week of the psalter are as follows:

Psalter week	Sunday of the Year / Week of the Year, of Lent or Advent
1	1, 5, 9, 13, 17, 21, 25, 29, 33
2	2, 6, 10, 14, 18, 22, 26, 30, 34
3	3, 7, 11, 15, 19, 23, 27, 31
4	4, 8, 12, 16, 20, 24, 28, 32

What Markers do I need ?

There are various different ways of bringing together information from several different parts of your Office book for the hour which you pray. The system I recommend to start with, is to make a series of bookmarks, one for each section of your book. Label them with the section of the book in which they will be used e.g:

FRT	for Frequently Recurring Text
4WP	for Four-week Psalter
NP	for Night Prayer Psalter
SY	for season of the year
SUN	for Sunday of the Year
CAL	for Feast (General/National Calendar or Solemnity)
COM	for Common
HY	for Hymn
MA	for Marian Anthem

If you already have a book with a series of ribbons in your book you may prefer to label these. You won't need all of them for each hour, but it helps to build up a good habit of preparing sections you are going to need at any given time.

Now try a simple Evening Prayer. Suppose it is Wednesday 27th October and last Sunday was the 30th Sunday of the Church's year. Where do you start?

The first check to make is to look at a calendar which contains Saints' feasts to see if one falls on this day. Each diocese publishes a book called an Ordo which contains these. If you are keen and want to be in line with your diocese, ask about them, otherwise use a daily missal or weekly newsletter from church.) On this particular day there is no saint commemorated. The next question is "What week of the Four-week psalter is it?" From the details given previously you know that it is week 2 of the psalter.

For this Evening Prayer you need only two markers, One for the Frequently Recurring Texts (FRT) and the other for the Four Week Psalter (4WP)

Setting the Markers

Place the FRT marker in the FRT section where the "Introduction to Each Hour" is given, and the 4WP marker on "Week 2 Wednesday Evening Prayer" in the Four-week Psalter section. You are ready to start!

Try to follow the indications for the markers to find your place in your book, then the actual text which you will be praying, the first phrase of which is given in the right hand column below. A change of number in the instructions indicates a switch of marker. The sequence goes like this:

1. FRT marker for the Introduction

(STAND) Introduction	**"O God come to our aid ... etc."**

2. 4WP marker

Hymn for Evening Prayer	**"O Trinity of blessed light ..."**
then first Antiphon,	**"We are waiting in hope ..."**
(SIT)	
then the first psalm (*Psalm* 61),	**"In God alone ..."**
then the Glory be... ,	
then the Antiphon again.	**"We are waiting in hope ..."**
(PAUSE for reflection)	
then second Antiphon	**"Let God bless us ..."**
then second psalm (*Psalm* 66),	**"O God be gracious ..."**
then Glory be... ,	

then second Antiphon again.	**"Let God bless us ..."**
(PAUSE for reflection)	
then third Antiphon,	**"All things were created ..."**
then Canticle,	**"Let us give thanks ..."**
then Glory be... ,	
third Antiphon again	**"All things were created ..."**
(PAUSE for reflection)	
Scripture Reading (*1 Pt* 5:5b-7)	**"Wrap yourselves in humility ..."**
(PAUSE)	
Short Responsory Response	**"Guard us Lord ..."**
Response repeated,	**"Guard us Lord ..."**
Verse	**"Hide us in ..."**
Response repeated	**"Guard us Lord ..."**
Glory be *(first half)*	**"Glory be to the Father and to the Son and to the Holy Spirit"**
Response repeated	**"Guard us Lord ..."**
(STAND)	
Magnificat Antiphon...	**"Show the power..."**

3. Turn to FRT marker

(The Magnificat may be a couple of pages further on ... turn to it)

Magnificat *(Start with sign of the cross)*	**"My soul glorifies the Lord ..."**
Glory be	**"Glory be ..."**

4. Turn back to 4WP marker

Magnificat Antiphon, repeat	**"Show the power ..."**
then Intercessions	**"At the end of the day ..."**

5. Turn again to FRT

Introduce the Our Father	**"Let us now pray ..."**
Pray the Our Father	**"Our Father ..."**

6. Turn to 4WP for the concluding Prayer

Concluding Prayer	**"Lord God, whose name ..."**

7. Turn to FRT for the Conclusion of the Hours

Conclusion - either	**"The Lord be with you ..."**
or	**"The Lord bless us ..."**

Evening Prayer (without finishing with a Marian Anthem) is then complete.

Flipping from one part of the book to another seven times may seem excessive for the simplest Evening prayer. It is. Within a short time introductions and conclusions will be learned. They are easy to remember. You will find yourself needing to go to the FRTs only once or twice, perhaps not at all if you have the Magnificat prayer on a card or on the back page of your Office book. At this stage praying with a group who pray it regularly, is a great help. Don't give up.

What Happens on a Sunday?

For Evening Prayer on Sunday during the Church's year (weeks 1 to 34) you would also need your "Sun" marker in the right Sunday of the "Sundays of the Year" section. You would use it for the Magnificat antiphon and concluding Prayer... otherwise as above. Remember that each week there are two Evening Prayers of Sunday... one on the Saturday evening (Sunday 1) and one on the Sunday Evening (Sunday 2).

What Happens in Lent ?

For Evening Prayer in Lent you would need your SY marker in the correct place in Lent in the "Seasons of the Year" section. This gives you different reading, intercessions etc. If you have a lenten hymn section put your Hy marker there and find a lenten hymn to use. Be careful to use the lenten Antiphons, (and miss out any

Alleluias), and use Lenten Psalms and canticles if they occur in the 4WP section.

What Happens on a Saint's Day ?

Saint's days come in three types:

1. Major Solemnities ... Here the Evening before is treated as part of the celebration. All the possible prayers from the Proper of Saints are used (CAL marker). Sometimes the saint's proper may also instruct you to use the Commons (COM marker).

2. Feasts ... Here the Evening before (vigil) does not become part of the celebration. The only Evening prayer of the Feast is the one on the actual day. This still may have its own proper (CAL), and may use a common (COM).

3. Memoria ... Here usually only the Magnificat Antiphon and concluding prayer are of the saint, all else from the Four-week psalter. (Memorias are often optional)

From the above it is obvious that some working-out and setting of markers is essential, at least while learning the ropes, where there is anything out of the ordinary in the day's celebration. Don't worry if you seem to get it wrong... prayer is still prayer!

Marian Anthem

It is common to conclude either Evening Prayer or Night Prayer with a short hymn to Our Lady (a final anthem to the Blessed Virgin). If you wish to do this at Evening Prayer find this section, mark it with your MA marker, and sing the anthem right at the end of Evening Prayer.

When you become used to the arrangement of the sections in your book then you can replace the section markers with unlabelled ribbons, prayer cards, or whatever else. Meanwhile keep using them until you know which section of the book is where.

This concludes the understanding of the sections, the building-blocks of which your Office book is made. By now you should have a good idea of what sections there are in your book, and what you might expect to find in each.

Exercises

1. Which week of the Four-week psalter would you use for:
   a. 2nd week of Advent?
   b. 17th Sunday of the Church's Year?
   c. 5th week of Lent?

2. How many different ways are there of commemorating a Saint's day using Evening prayer? What are the differences?

3. What different sections of your book would you need to include for the second Sunday in Lent and for the second Sunday in the Church's Year ?

4. From memory put the following in correct order for Evening Prayer: Magnificat, 1st psalm, Hymn, New Testament Canticle, 2nd Psalm, Intercessions, Scripture reading, Short Responsory, Our Father.

LESSON 4

Morning Prayer and Night Prayer

Having started to come to grips with Evening Prayer, much of the procedure for praying Morning Prayer and Night Prayer will follow quite easily.

Morning Evening and Night prayer have a similar structure of hymn, Psalms, canticles etc. The main differences between Morning Prayer and Evening Prayer are as follows:

1. If Morning Prayer is the first hour of the day it can be preceded by the Invitatory Antiphon and Psalm, (as mentioned previously).

2. The sequence of Psalms and non-gospel canticle is slightly changed from that in Evening Prayer. Because the non-gospel canticle is from the Old Testament in Morning Prayer rather than the New Testament it is situated between the two Psalms rather than after them.

3. Celebrations of Feasts and Solemnities often use the Psalms and Canticles of Sunday Week 1, rather than

those of the week and day of the four-week psalter. (Some Office books provide a sheet with the Psalms and canticles for week 1 Sunday Morning, to avoid having to flip back too often to the four week psalter.)

4. On Sundays of week 1 and week 3 the Old Testament canticle contains a doxology (it gives glory to the Trinity) in the last verse, so whenever this canticle is used an exception is made to the usual practice of ending with a Glory be...

Morning Prayer

Suppose it is Friday today, and last Sunday was the 17th Sunday. Let us suppose too that it is not a Saint's day today.

Setting Your Markers

As with an easy Evening Prayer there will be only two markers needed, the same two. The first of these is in the Frequently Recurring Texts section. If it is the first hour of the day then instead of being sited at the "Introduction to each hour" heading, it should instead be at the "Introduction to the Daily Office" section, usually found right at the beginning of the Frequently Recurring Texts section of your Office book. Put your FRT marker in the correct position.

The second marker needs to go in the Four-week Psalter section.

From previous details you know that week 17 of the Church's year uses the 1st week of the psalter cycle. Look in this section in your book, and put your 4WP marker at the start of Week 1 Friday Morning Prayer. You are ready to start!

Starting to pray

1. FRT marker for the Introduction

(*STAND*)
(*making a sign of the cross on your lips as you say it*)

"O Lord open my lips ..."

Then follows the Invitatory Antiphon, which can either be in FRT or in 4WP section... check to see where it is,

"Give thanks to the Lord ..."

Next comes your choice of Invitatory psalm from FRT,

e.g. "Come ring out our joy ..."

then Glory be...
then Invitatory Antiphon again.

"Give thanks to the Lord ..."

2. From your 4WP marker pray the hymn

Hymn for Morning Prayer	**"We bless you Father ..."**
then first Antiphon	**"Lord you will be pleased ..."**
then first psalm,	**"Have mercy on me, God ..."**
then Glory be then first Antiphon again,	**"Lord you will be pleased ..."**
(PAUSE) then second Antiphon,	**"All the descendants of Israel ..."**
then Canticle,	**"Truly, God of Israel ..."**
then Glory be,	
then second Antiphon again,	**"All the descendants of Israel ..."**
(PAUSE) then third Antiphon,	**"Come before the Lord ..."**
then the second psalm,	**"Cry out with joy to the Lord ..."**
then the Glory be, then the third Antiphon again,	**"Come before the Lord ..."**

(PAUSE)

then the Short Reading, (*Ep* 4:29-32) then the Short Responsory, Response	**"Do not use harmful words ..."** **"In the morning ..."**
Response repeated,	**"In the morning ..."**
Verse,	**"Make me know the way"**
Response repeated,	**"In the morning ..."**
then	**"Glory be to the Father and to the Son and to the Holy Spirit"**
Response repeated,	**"In the morning ..."**
(STAND)	
then the Gospel canticle,	**"The Lord has visited ..."**

3. Then turn to FRT marker

(The Benedictus may be a couple of pages further on ... turn to it)

Benedictus *(Start with sign of the cross)*	**"Blessed be the Lord ..."**
Glory be	**"Glory be ..."**

4. Then turn back to 4WP marker

Benedictus Antiphon repeat	**"The Lord has visited ..."**
then the Intercessions.	**"Lord Jesus Christ ..."**

5. Turn again to FRT

Introduce the Our Father	**"Let us now pray ..."**
Pray the Our Father	**"Our Father ..."**

6. Turn to 4WP for the concluding Prayer,

Concluding Prayer	**"Lord God, you ..."**

7. Turn to FRT for the Conclusion of the Hours.

Conclusion - either	**"The Lord be with you ..."**
or	**"The Lord bless us ..."**
(Without the Invitatory)	

(To pray Morning Prayer without the Invitatory start in the
FRT section in the same place as you did for Evening Prayer

"O God come to our aid ..."

All the rest is identical from points 2 to 7 as above.)

Sundays, Seasons, Saints etc.

All of the markers which you use for the Evening Prayer hours are the same as those used for the Morning.

Once you have mastered the process for praying Evening Prayer the extra which has to be learned in order to pray Morning Prayer is very little, and vice versa.

Night Prayer

Night prayer is similar to Morning and Evening, but simpler to pray than either. It has no intercessions, no canticle other than the gospel *Nunc dimittis*, and no Our Father. It needs less flipping back to the FRT section.

Just as Sunday has two sets of Evening Prayer (one on the Saturday evening and one on the Sunday) so it is with Night Prayer. Solemnities are treated in the same way as Sundays and use the same Night Prayers as a Sunday. There are no special prayers for different times or seasons other than missing out any Alleluias in Lent, and those responsories which are included in the weekly Night Prayer Psalmody section.

Hymns

Night prayer has its own set of hymns, and you should be familiar with this section in your Office book. Unlike Morning and Evening Prayer this is not sung immediately after the introduction. What takes place here is an examination of conscience (using any way which you have found effective) and any penitential rite [many people use one from the Mass e.g. 'I confess...', 'Lord have mercy...'. etc.]

Setting Your Markers

You will need three markers for your Night prayer (or four if you are concluding with your Marian Anthem).

The first marker is your FRT marker, placed at the same heading " Introduction to each hour" as for Evening Prayer. Once you have found your hymns for Night prayer choose one and put your 'Hy' marker there. Put your 'NP' marker in the Night Prayer psalter section on the day in question. A typical Sequence would be for Monday Night Prayer:

1. FRT marker for the Introduction

(STAND)
Introduction   **"O God come to our aid ..."**

2. Examination of Conscience, privately, using whatever texts you want from wherever. Then any penitential rite or prayers you choose as mentioned above.

3. Then NP marker (for Monday Night Prayer)

For first Antiphon	"You, Lord God ..."
Psalm,	"Turn your ear, O Lord ..."
Glory be...	
first Antiphon again,	"You, Lord God ..."
(PAUSE)	
Scripture Reading (*1 Th* 5:9-10)	"God chose us ..."
(PAUSE)	
Short Responsory Response,	"Into your hands, Lord ..."
response repeated,	"Into your hands, Lord ..."
verse,	"You have redeemed us ..."
response repeated,	"Into your hands, Lord ..."
then,	"Glory be to the Father and to the Son and to the Holy Spirit"
response repeated,	"Into your hands, Lord ..."

(STAND)

Antiphon,	**"Save us, Lord ..."**
Nunc Dimittis *(Start with sign of the cross)*	**"At last, all-powerful master ..."**
then,	**"Glory be ..."**
antiphon,	**"Save us, Lord ..."**
concluding prayer,	**"Lord, give our bodies restful sleep ..."**

4. Then FRT marker for the Night Prayer Blessing

Blessing	**"The lord grant us a quiet night ..."**

(If a Marian Anthem is used, as with Evening Prayer it is sung at the end.)

This concludes Night Prayer.

Second psalm

A second psalm, (with preceding antiphon, Glory be, second antiphon and pause), occurs on Saturday [= Sunday 1], and Wednesday night only ... all others have only one Psalm.)

Short Responsory of Night Prayer may vary with the season. This is shown in the Night Prayer Psalter when it does.

This concludes our brief look at the Hours of Morning Prayer and Night prayer. When marking-up your book don't worry if you can't find all the sections, or whether you have got everything right. Don't worry either if everything is not yet crystal clear just from working through this tutorial. Many things become clear with time and by praying with others.

Exercises

1. Put your markers in the right places in your book for Morning Prayer on the Feast of the Assumption

2. When is the 'Glory be', not said after a canticle?

3. Put your markers in your book for Night prayer if it is the Solemnity of the Assumption tomorrow.

4. When would you sing a Marian Anthem?

LESSON 5

Understanding the Printed Psalter Page

During the summer I visited an indoor sports hall. No sports were being played there at the time. On the floor were a collection of lines, obviously marking out various playing areas or pitches for different sports. They were marked in different colours and I spent some time working out which was for badminton, which for basketball and wondering for which sport the other marked playing area might be.

The same feeling, comes to me when I look at a printed page of the Four-Week Psalter section. In addition to the printed words are several sets of symbols whose meaning is not obvious. This lesson aims to help show their meaning and use.

Information in this lesson is not essential. You can pray and join in the hours without knowing any of it. Hopefully it will, however, satisfy some curiosity and help you to feel more at ease when praying the hours. It may also help you to get the most out of the book in reciting or singing the Psalms.

Psalm Numbering

When the Bible was first translated from Hebrew to Greek the grouping of different verses into Psalms was slightly changed. For this reason many of the Psalms are referred to not by one number, but by two, depending on whether the bible from which they were taken has been translated from the Hebrew or the Greek (the Septuagint) version.

For most of the Psalms the Greek Septuagint version number is one less than the Hebrew number. The relationship between the different numbering is given below:

Greek Septuagint Number	Hebrew Number
1 - 8	1 - 8
9	9 - 10
10 - 112	11 -113
113114 - 115	
114 - 115	116
116 - 145	117 - 146
146 - 147	147
148 - 150	148 - 150

In the Psalter where there are two numberings. The lower Greek Septuagint number is given first, followed by the Hebrew number.

There are also differences in the numbering of the scriptural verses between different bibles, but as no detailed numbering of verses is given in the Psalter this is something which we do not need to be aware of in the Office.

Antiphons with Daggers

Open your Office book at the Four-week Psalter section and turn to the Psalter for Week 1 Saturday Morning Prayer. Go to the third antiphon (i.e. for the second Psalm).

The antiphon is "O Praise the Lord all you nations." On the printed page immediately after this antiphon you will see a small dagger!

The plot thickens as you look to the psalm and see a similar dagger to the left of the second line of the psalm.

What is its meaning?

These daggers, which are linked to antiphons are there to draw your attention to the fact that the antiphon verse is the same as the first line of the psalm which it accompanies. This happens quite frequently in the psalter. Where this occurs this phrase is not said, or sung, twice, but only once. Because the antiphon is the first line of the psalm , the prayer goes from the antiphon to the second line of the psalm, rather than repeating the first. i.e.

Antiphon: **"O praise the Lord, all you nations"**

Psalm continues: **"acclaim him all ..."**

Verses

The word 'verse' when we look at the psalter can have two different meanings. If you are used to reading poetry or singing songs then to you a verse is a group of lines together on a printed page. In the English language editions of the psalter these are not the same as the scriptural verses. We need to make the distinction and call the blocks of text on the psalter page 'stanzas'. Usually a stanza in the English language psalter consists of more than one scriptural verse.

In the Latin psalter stanzas would usually be printed in accordance with scriptural verses, though if the verse was very long then a scriptural verse may be split into two stanzas. This was to help the singing or chant. The singing of these verses was usually a simple tone of two short phrases. It is still common today in some communities to sing the psalter psalms not by large stanzas (using several phrases of music), but by their shorter stanzas (usually scriptural verses) keeping to a simple two-line chant.

If you wish to do this you have to be able to work out where these smaller verses should begin and end. There are three symbols on the printed page which enable you to do this.

They are:
1. The asterisk at the end of a psalm-line
2. The dagger at the end of a psalm-line
3. The 'brace', a curved line to the left of a particular psalm-line joining it to another psalm line in a stanza above or below.

For an example of how each of these work, turn to your Four-Week Psalter section for Week 1 Monday Morning, and go to the second psalm [Psalm 28 (29)]

The Asterisk

The first stanza of the Psalm contains four lines. If you look in a bible you will see that it contains two scriptural verses, the first two lines being the first verse, and the next two lines being the second. The norm is to have each scriptural verse represented by two printed lines in the psalter. The asterisk marks the mid-point of this small verse. If a two-line psalm tone is used to chant the psalm, it is here that the first musical phrase is completed, and the second is about to begin. The asterisk can be thought of as marking the hinge at the centre of the small verse of the Psalm.

Where an asterisk is used in a canticle it has a similar meaning, that of indicating the hinge-point if sung to a two-line chant. Here again it usually, but not always, indicates the half-way point of a scriptural verse. If you look at the canticle for the same hour, Week 1 Monday Morning, you will spot this latter case. Here the stanzas are grouped according to the scriptural verses. The fourth stanza, however, is longer than the average scriptural verse. The editors have split it in two (going by the asterisks), so that it would take two simple two-line tones to chant, though it is only one scriptural verse.

The dagger at the end

In both psalms and canticles often the first half of the small verse is not the same length as the second one. If you look again at the canticle for Monday Week 1 Morning Prayer you have a good example. In the first two stanzas the first 'half' is longer than the second half, and the first half takes up two lines, whereas the second half takes up only one. Note that in each case there is a dagger at the end of the line. This dagger serves two purposes:

To let you know that the line which precedes it is part of the initial phrase for a two-line psalm tone.

To indicate to anyone who wants to sing this using a simple tone that it is an extra group of words to be fitted-in at the beginning of the first half of the tone.

In practice this would usually mean that it was sung on a single note, and the melody of the first part

of the chant took over on the next line, which
concludes with the asterisk.

The brace

If you look at the same Morning Prayer and Psalm 28
(29) once more and go to the end of the third stanza and
beginning of the fourth you will see a brace. This line at
the left of the Psalm line links it to whichever other line it
belongs to in order to be used with the simple chant.

Gelineau and Grail Stanzas and accents

Some years ago a new French bible was translated, the
forerunner of the English 'Jerusalem Bible'. In it an
attempt was made to group the Psalm stanzas not
according to the Latin, but rather according to the pattern
and rhythm of the original Hebrew. Father Gelineau wrote
a set of Psalm tones intended to bring out this Hebrew
rhythm, which has a regular stress pattern, or beat, in the
Psalm stanzas. This ideal has been carried on in the
English Grail version of the Psalms, which is used for the
Office psalters. The indication of the point of stress is
given by an accent (pointing). The norm for different
Psalms may be lines with 2 stresses, 3 stresses or 4
stresses, or a pattern of these which repeats through the
Psalm. Father Gelineau composed a set of tones for

general use with these Psalms and in addition wrote specific tones for specific Psalms. Both of these are available and used in the Grail version of Psalms. The "standard" tones are found in the back of the book of the singing version of the Grail Psalms, and the specific tones are available in publications of the Grail. Both of these take account of irregular-length stanzas.

In practice many communities will use psalm tones which are a compromise between the Gelineau tones and the simple two-line tones, and so will pay attention. to different daggers, asterisks, accents etc. depending on the nature of the tones which are chosen.

Exercises

1. What are the following for?
   a. asterisk
   b. brace
   c. dagger
   d. accent

2. Why are there two numbers which can represent one Psalm?

3. What does a dagger after an antiphon indicate?

LESSON 6

Enhancing your Prayer

This lesson looks at ways to vary, personalise, and thoughtfully use the different elements of the hours. In so doing may you praise God more fervently, be nourished by his Word more fruitfully, and be present more attentively in prayer. Not all ways of praise and prayer fit each person. Always look to improve your prayer. Don't be afraid to try other methods, but at the same time don't think that there is anything wrong if any particular way of prayer doesn't feel right or comfortable.

Hymns

Hymns are intended to be sung. If you don't know a melody that belongs to a particular hymn try to find one. If you can't, then use another hymn which you find easier. The tradition, particularly for praise, of human expression by song rather than the spoken word, is great. In sung praise we express the sentiment with more of ourselves than when we speak it.

If you have weak voices try using an instrument, or a tape as backing for your singing. If the group can't sing then perhaps an individual could sing solo. If no-one can

sing then it may be worth looking at religious poetry,
(some Office books contain sections of poems).

Antiphons, Psalms and Canticles

Like hymns these should be sung. It was never the
intention that they should be spoken. As with anything
else it is good to start simply. If you are not used to
singing anything, perhaps start with a sung Magnificat
from a hymnbook, or a sung hymn or Marian Anthem
before progressing to further music.

If you are uncertain about using psalm-tones a good
guide is to attempt to use one with which you are already
familiar. Often at parish Sunday Masses the Responsorial
Psalm will be sung. If this is the case then a familiar tone
from one of these might be good to start with. Failing this
there are cassette tapes available of Psalms. Another
alternative is to recite Psalms accompanied by music.

Whether they are sung or spoken, there are different
ways of praying them. The most common way is with one
person in the group introducing each part of the hour, then
the group splitting into two (sometimes called two choirs)
and each group reciting alternate stanzas, coming together
to recite the antiphon after each Psalm and canticle.

In some reflective groups it is common to have a
lengthy PAUSE after each Psalm and canticle, during

which any member can repeat, out loud, any phrase which has made an impression on them.

Sometimes we find ourselves praying sad Psalms when we don't feel sad and joyful Psalms when we don't feel joyful. These are good occasions to remind ourselves that when we pray the hour, the Prayer of the Church, we are more than just one individual. As the body of Christ I "Rejoice with those who rejoice and am sad with those in sorrow" (*Rm* 12:15)

Psalms, Israel and Christian Prayer

The Psalms are the prayer-book of the people of Israel. Each has its place in the celebrations and the disappointments of life. It is helpful to reflect on their purpose.

When the psalter was revised it was intended that at the end of each Psalm there would be a short reflection which could be read, which would help those who pray the Psalms to interpret them from a Christian perspective (called a 'Psalm Prayer'). These are present in the American editions of Office books. The UK editions came out before these prayers were completed. Psalm Prayers for the Psalms of Morning Prayer and Evening Prayer have recently been published by Veritas in Ireland and are available in the UK. If you don't have access to them try spending some time thinking where the people of Israel would have used a particular Psalm, and how that particular Psalm is relevant to Christian life.

Intercessions

The printed intercessions in the Office each consist of two phrases so that either the second half may be used as a response, or a uniform response may be spoken after both phrases of the intercession have been spoken. Extra intercessions are encouraged. If these are at Evening Prayer, the best place for them is before the final intercession, which is for the dead. If at Morning Prayer extra intercessions can go anywhere.

Using such intercessions is a good easy way to make the hours more personal. Two suggestions to help are as follows:

1. Pray for your friends using a list or address book, an alphabetical list, with one letter of the alphabet each day fits easily into the 4-week cycle of the psalter, leaving space for a few special intentions to make it up to the 28 days.

2. Keep a list of important dates, anniversaries, etc. with the calendar you use to check if there is a Saint's day to remember, or in your Office book in the proper of Saints. Pray for and remember these dates each year as you pray the Office.

These are not the only possibilities. Perhaps praying for particular intentions on a weekly cycle would suit your group better?

Never stop growing

The regular habit of praying the hours is a great strength. Such habits carry us through the bad patches, and build our confidence in the good.

What is to be avoided is that they become so much 'habit' that the words come out without thought, without feeling and without personal intent.

Try to regularly look at the different parts of the hours, and ask "How can I pray this better?", or "How can I use variety to refresh prayer life?". This is a practice which builds on the habit which is simply routine, refreshes it and provides further blessings.

Exercises

1. What is a Psalm Prayer?

2. Discuss different ways in which Psalms can be prayed.

3. Make a plan to help incorporate your personal or group intercessions into the Office hours.